The *'i'* Problem Theory

The *'i'* Problem Theory
Solve your problems

Anthony Robinski

Copyright © 2025 by Anthony Robinski

All rights reserved. No part of this publication may be reproduced, distributed, or transmitted in any form or by any means, including, photocopying, recording, or other electronic or mechanical methods, without the prior written permission of the copyright owner and the publisher, except in the case of brief quotations embodied in critical reviews and certain other noncommercial uses permitted by copyright law. For permission requests, write to the publisher, addressed "Attention: Permissions Coordinator," at the address below.

ARPress
45 Dan Road Suite 15
Canton MA 02021
 Hotline: 1(888) 821-0229
 Fax: 1(508) 545-7580

Ordering Information:
Quantity sales. Special discounts are available on quantity purchases by corporations, associations, and others. For details, contact the publisher at the address above.

Printed in the United States of America.

 ISBN-13:   Softcover   979-8-89676-469-4
            eBook   979-8-89676-470-0

Library of Congress Control Number: 2026900312

Preface

    I asked my brother why the world was turning on itself and why people, in general, were becoming so hateful. People are hurting others in the name of "something" or for the sake of hurting others. What can be done to help people solve their problems and help them not to be so hateful? My brother told me he did not have a reasonable answer but would take it upon himself to find one. As I waited, I contemplated the answer to my question. One day, as I was running, the answer came to me in the form of an equation. The equation does not define a person's specific problems but how the person could find a universal solution to overcome the problems. If one individual can help themselves, that individual becomes one less person to worry about and one less hateful person to harm others.

    The theory behind the equation can handle almost any problem a person may face and assist them in improving themselves while moving forward. The equation allows the individual to go from having a problem (<)to finding their problem (=)to becoming greater than their problem (>). At any point, greater than problems (>) can become problems again because life is always moving forward and has a way of testing our resolve. Luck is not a factor because we can improve ourselves and become greater than our problems.

However pleasant it is to be lucky, it is unwise to count on blind luck when we are the ones who can create our own version of luck. The only guarantee in life is that which we do.

So, my brother, the answer to my question is "The i problem theory." I hope you agree that this mathematical equation is enough of an answer to satisfy the question in all of its unknown infinite wisdom—a simple equation to solve simple to complicated life problems. If a person can solve their problems, they may be less likely to want to hurt others.

The Equation
$$X + i \times (n \times O) = Y$$

There are three situations that must be identified:

a) Problem > Y (you have a problem that is affecting you)
b) Problem = Y (you have identified the problem)
c) Problem + L < Y (you have overcome the problem, and it no longer affects you)

$\underline{X}$ represents inheritance, what family you were born into, where you were born, your parents and what they teach you, how much money they have, and all the factors individuals cannot control when they are born.

$\underline{i}$ represents the individual; what you can do, how you think, your capabilities as a person, the money you have, and all factors concerning you and your situation.

$\underline{n}$ represents information; all information that can be learned, acquired, computed, or leveraged.

$\underline{O}$ represents others, other people, and what they can do, what they know, and where they are.

$\underline{Y}$ represents the mathematically combined efforts of **X**, *i*, *n*, and O. The strength of why you do something to be better than a problem.

$\underline{L}$ represents life, the factors of life that make overcoming a problem difficult.

When faced with a problem and the situation is (Problem > Y), you still have a problem affecting you. It would be best if you increased your Y to stop the problem from affecting you, and the best way to do that is to increase your *i* (individual capabilities), *n* (information), and O (others). Leveraging these factors can increase the effectiveness of your Y. As adults, **X** becomes less of a factor because it can only add to your Y. A higher **X** may be helpful throughout life; however, most problems are overcome by increasing *n* and O, which are leveraged against the value of *i*.

You have identified the problem if the situation is (Problem = Y). You know what factors need to change to improve your Y, bringing you closer to overcoming the problem. Getting to this point means you have learned how to improve yourself and your situation. Keep working on improving the Y.

When the situation reaches (Problem +L < Y), you overcome the problem and are no longer affected by it. The problem never goes away; you just become greater than the problem preventing it from affecting you.

X is bold and capital because that is not something an individual can change. *i* and *n* are lowercase because they are inputs an individual can control, increasing or decreasing. O and Y are uppercase because they cannot be controlled, but their values can change based on an individual's actions.

No inputs are negative because things either add value to your Y or do not. i and n are the two most important factors in identifying any problem. For more significant problems, you will need to leverage the power of O to overcome them.

-Robinski, Anthony

An Example

An individual is faced with whether to buy a house or not. This situation can be more emotional than objective, considering how much owning a home could mean to a person on an intrinsic level. Using the *i* problem theory can be used in this situation.

First, we have **X**, which would be your current cash on hand or other liquidity, and this is what you are going into the problem with. Let's assume the house costs three hundred thousand dollars, and your current **X** is only twenty-four thousand. At first, it may seem that you cannot afford a house, but before a decision is made, the questions that need to be addressed are, "should" you buy a house, or "can" you buy a house? You are at Problem > Y.

To overcome the problem of determining which is the best question to ask, increasing your *i* is the easiest thing you can do, considering you have the most control over it. The decision is made to change spending habits to lower the money leaving accounts, save more on paychecks, and change to a more aggressive investment strategy. After all these inputs have been calculated, the total dollar value is now thirty thousand dollars. There is an understanding that thirty thousand is less than three hundred thousand dollars, but there is still that desire to own that home.

The next thing to do would be to increase *n*, which would be information. After spending a few hours researching, the information gained boils down to a few questions that can be answered to gauge whether someone should buy a house. The questions are; can you put down twenty percent of the home's value, is the mortgage going to be more than thirty percent of your income, assuming it's stable, and do you have good credit?

The current situation with the thirty thousand dollars, the excellent credit, and the overall estimated mortgage is less than thirty percent of your monthly income based on an online tool you have. You "can" buy a house. Considering three hundred thousand dollars is much money, and you will be paying for it for the next fifteen to thirty years, it is not a decision to be made lightly, so more information is needed.

But raw information is not enough to decide, so it would be best to talk to the experts and increase your O. After visiting a few banks and mortgage lenders, over half of them say you are in an excellent position to purchase a house. You are now at Problem = Y. Can you buy a house? Yes, you can. But this only means you have identified the problem and not overcome it. That would be the L factor, the life factor, something institutions may not be able to consider because they do not know a customer's behaviors.

At this point, all information you gain will be factual-based and not life-based. The complexity of gathering enough information on your own and consulting experts may not give you insight into the reality of buying a home. It would be best to talk to people who already own homes. You consult friends, family, co-workers, and social media. On the other side of buying a house, you discover some drawbacks; you have to pay taxes on the property, cover maintenance, insurance, Homeowners association fees, and furnish the place. You are responsible for the entire property.

Some of the benefits, though, are that you can turn the property into a passive source of income, meaning you receive money without needing to do labor. You can hire a property manager to handle maintenance, and the property can generate a profit once the mortgage has been paid off. It can increase your net worth and give you access to equity which can be leveraged. In ten to fifteen years, you could have increased your passive income stream by almost two hundred percent if you had studied the process of using real estate to generate income. Nothing great in life is achieved without much enduring.

You have arrived at Problem + L < Y with all these factors. You no longer need to ask yourself if you "should" buy a house or if you "can" buy a house. You know the answer to both questions. Using the i problem theory, you have removed bias and emotional thought to come to a reasonable conclusion. Using the equation help you to navigate to complexities of how to solve a problem using simple math.

The next time you are faced with a decision, look at the equation to help you navigate the path to your answer. If you do not understand the example given after reading this, you should consider improving your i and n.

Problem: _____

X: (What you have)

_____

_____

i: (You can add more to yourself as you work through the problem)

_____

_____

_____

n: (What information can you learn, find, discover)

_____

_____

O: (Other people)

_____

L: (Problems that arose while attempting to solve the problem)

_____

_____

The 'i' Problem Theory

Problem: _____

X: (What you have)

_____

_____

i: (You can add more to yourself as you work through the problem)

_____

_____

_____

n: (What information can you learn, find, discover)

_____

_____

O: (Other people)

_____

L: (Problems that arose while attempting to solve the problem)

_____

_____

Problem: _____

X: (What you have)

_____

_____

i: (You can add more to yourself as you work through the problem)

_____

_____

_____

n: (What information can you learn, find, discover)

_____

_____

O: (Other people)

_____

L: (Problems that arose while attempting to solve the problem)

_____

_____

Problem: _____

X: (What you have)

_____

_____

i: (You can add more to yourself as you work through the problem)

_____

_____

_____

n: (What information can you learn, find, discover)

_____

_____

O: (Other people)

_____

L: (Problems that arose while attempting to solve the problem)

_____

_____

Problem: _____

X: (What you have)

_____

_____

i: (You can add more to yourself as you work through the problem)

_____

_____

_____

n: (What information can you learn, find, discover)

_____

_____

O: (Other people)

_____

L: (Problems that arose while attempting to solve the problem)

_____

_____

Problem: _____

X: (What you have)

_____

_____

i: (You can add more to yourself as you work through the problem)

_____

_____

_____

n: (What information can you learn, find, discover)

_____

_____

O: (Other people)

_____

L: (Problems that arose while attempting to solve the problem)

_____

_____

Problem: _____

X: (What you have)

_____

_____

i: (You can add more to yourself as you work through the problem)

_____

_____

_____

n: (What information can you learn, find, discover)

_____

_____

O: (Other people)

_____

L: (Problems that arose while attempting to solve the problem)

www.ingramcontent.com/pod-product-compliance
Lightning Source LLC
Chambersburg PA
CBHW060609030426
42337CB00019B/3683